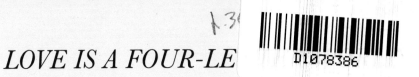

LOVE IS A FOUR-LE

Literature

.. .. .Y LIBRARY

by the same poet:

Slipping The Tugs (Lincolnshire & Humberside Arts, 1982)
This Day Dawning (Peterloo Poets, 1989)

Love is a Four-Letter World

Maurice Rutherford

PETERLOO POETS

First published in 1994
by Peterloo Poets
2 Kelly Gardens, Calstock, Cornwall PL18 9SA, U.K.

16/3/95

01822 - 833473

**A catalogue record for this book is available
from the British Library**

ISBN 1-871471-43-5

Printed in Great Britain by
Latimer Trend & Company Ltd, Plymouth

ACKNOWLEDGEMENTS are due to the editors of the following journals and anthologies: *Acumen, Bogg, Critical Survey, Envoi, The Green Book, Insight (Scunthorpe Star), Iota, Iron, London Magazine, Orbis, Other Poetry, Outposts, Pennine Platform, Poetry & Audience, Poetry Durham, Poetry Nottingham, Poetry Review, Proof, Prospice, The Rialto, Scratch, Staple, Vision On, Voices Aloud.*

The author is especially grateful to the many without whose encouragement, support, or simply *being there* the poems in this collection might not have occurred.

For Olive

—and to those many

'For love all love of other sights controls,
And makes one little room an everywhere.'

Contents

A Silence

What I remember remembering
of nights he came home drunk to her
is not the thump of a falling chair
or the shock of shattering glass,
not the strop of strident voice on voice
that rattled the sash in its frame,

but the way a silence held the house
between each charge and countercharge —
the ache as I lay and raised my head
off the pillow till the neck-muscles gave —
and relief when their drubbing began again;
and how morning came, and he'd gone.

The Light Of The World

(a Holman Hunt print remembered)

Taller than I'd first imagined Jesus;
nor could I then be certain
the expression on his face
changed as light from his lamp

fell through tall cow-parsley
to the bare feet I feared for
on such harsh ground;
his hand knocking at the door.

His eyes tired, sad perhaps
as if he, too, would have preferred,
like my elder brother,
not to be made to share

a bedroom with a boy
so young who daily broke
the unfair tenth commandment
on such as seniority,

a waistcoatful of pockets,
full-length baggy flannels
and heavy-soled brown brogues.
And Brylcreemed hair

parted, sleek as the flakes
of kippers our father boned
when mother took them out
from the fireside oven

in brittle back-numbers
of *Hull Daily Mail*
cooked bronze as the kippers.
The hot, glazed bed-brick

she'd wrap and carry upstairs
to the foot of our bed
under the watchful eyes of Jesus.
My brother, two hours later to bed,

offering my offending socks
with his prayer to the night air,
trapping them under the sash.
Neither forgiving my trespass.

Bitter Aloes

With him, it was the whisky.
Thumb-sucking,
the children's shared addiction,
weaning themselves;
a family saying something
in bitten fingernails.

It was the whisky
tacked him against the tide
homeward at three for one
on the quiet Sundays
to the oven-dried lunch
and serenity he smashed
through the kitchen window.

And the short sleep to follow
brought him only the worse
to the evening's loud quarrel —
the children out of the way
between cold, clean sheets
to a bitter suckling.

Downstairs, her voice
bursting its bubbles
on the cracked ceiling;
and his, rumbling
in sudden deliveries
like Best York Cobbles
down the coalhouse wall.

Monday's breakfast in the draught
behind the kitchen curtains.
Back home from school at four
to the new glass pane,
we finger-printed putty
for posterity.

Sunday again and a fire
in the frontroom grate—
a new handcut crystal vase
elegant on the sideboard,
a promise yet unbroken—
the bright coals slipping.
With him, it was the whisky.

Peter's House

Peter's house was different.
No father home each evening
from the docks; an uncle
occasionally from sea.
There we could feel free.

Like when his uncle Jack
brought home the parrot.
'African Grey', he had said,
'screech like a windlass brake,
but can't get the bugger to talk.'

'Should have had its tongue
split with a sixpenny piece
when the bugger was young',
his uncle Jack had said.
One morning the parrot lay dead.

Landing in Hull, late summer,
he'd brought a chameleon.
Aloof, it had held a still pose
on top of the curtain pole —
it was there when we came in from school:

Peter, his uncle and I had caught flies
and pulled off one of their wings,
sent them climbing in range of its tongue.
'like feeding a donkey strawberries',
his uncle Jack had said, 'it is.'

And not very long after that
Peter's house had been ripped
from its roots by a bomb,
and I heard that his uncle Jack
had gone down off Murmansk.

Tutorial

What can I say of her face? It was all
of a smile; hair done in a tight-pinned bun;
her bosom ample, indeterminate.
Ageless, she had lived in this room always.

Her skirt wide, almost, as it was long,
you had to stand behind to see at all
the bentwood chair she sat on.
She was the sort that people came to.

Her gold-tipped teeth a fascination
glimpsed in the gas-light's surge
when the mantle prattled. She rummaged
in the chiffonier, its dark drawer of memories

and playing-cards, found the harmonica —
repaired at one end with a sharp twist
of wire saved from a firewood bundle.
It was a lesson in a simple language:

'blo-ow suck blo-ow suck blo-ow blow blo-ow',
teaching a boy's bloomed lips to mouth
her favourite and only tune
in a camphorated key of 'C'

in the dim-lit room, with her smile,
the gold, the spittle that they shared
and the one discordant reed
that made the song their own.

The Cod Farm

I have your photo on my wall
in grainy not-quite-black-and-white,
blown-up, to try to bring you close

the way few sons and fathers are.
The original's in Hull museum —
The Cod Farm: you, flat cap and all,

with cod spread out on racks to dry
salt-white, 'earning a crust' by which
Mum bought that first school uniform

I rolled around the playground in
to make less obviously new
to boys with bigger fists than mine.

'See Maurice, see our Dad again!'.
Quite what the others find of you
in me, they don't explain. Bald head;

the less than generous mouth; your voice?
And I don't tell them how I feel
a certain late affinity;

how, since you died, sometimes it seems
it's not my face but yours I shave
(though wrong way round); your faults I see

mirrored in me — like how I use
codology the way you did
for blowing up reality

in grainy not-quite-blacks-or-whites
to hold on to a love I fear
to lose, or maybe never had.

Solitaire

(i.m. Maud Evelyne and Evelyn)

Sometime before the start of World War One
there must have been a day when all their pride
reflected from the facets of one stone,
claw-mounted, on an eighteen-carat ring.
And later, newly wed, they would have stood,
she, with a centre-parting, combed-back hair
and he, head high, in stiff wing-collared shirt,
braced for the photograph's magnesium flare.

Filial wistfulness would beg the lie
that marriage, war, attrition of the years
exacted equal toll from each, but truth
insists that this was not the case, and cites
their ring she gave to me before she died,
its shank worn thin, the diamond vivified.

Woman In The Crowd

for Jean, in a slow winter

Your Mum and I down town —
new mall, old marketplace —
and in the shifting crowd
briefly, perhaps your face,
deportment, hair.

Two youngsters of your own,
with half a lifetime gone,
your home a world away
from home and moving on.
Yet here you are

where albums hold you still
freeze-framed along the years;
your paintings in our hall;
your laughter, letters, tears
wring in locked drawers;

and sometimes, in the folds
of dreams, a daughter's call —
we waken to your name —
a known kick on the wall
of the spent womb.

In Vacuo

I keep them in this box which used to house
five units each of fifty carbon sheets —
your postcards: Pyramids, the Nile and Dhows;
Playa de Palma; cafés on the streets

of Paris; gaudy panoramic views
from Naxos where you made a second home.
'Brazil is beautiful — I'm on a cruise
along the Amazon.' 'With love from Rome.'

In what we'd neither of us claim has been
a close relationship, these cards fill gaps;
each brings the beating of shared blood. Each scene
initiates a survey of my maps:

I pinpoint Casablanca — 'Oh, the heat!',
place Tarbert out on Harris — '... blowing hard ...',
and trace the many places where we meet
in words behind the gloss of each kept card

then hoard them tightly packed inside their box,
in vain to prove that your propensity
for travelling supports the paradox
of distance closing to propinquity.

Love Of An Autumn Afternoon

September sunshine cuts a wedge of green
and lays the cypress tree three times its length
along the lawn; the honeysuckled air
invigorates — like coming out from school.
It's on such afternoons as this I mean
to tell you of my love, how much its strength
has grown with time; to lean across your chair
and touch, and kiss you, lightly, hoping you'll
respond. And so I do — and you do, too,
and now our autumn's warm and green and gold.
True, there are days, not many but a few,
when friendliness and love remain untold,
but on such afternoons as this it's fair
to say there's nothing that we two won't share.

Mrs. Cholmondeley

Squeaks of a dry-hinged gate,
or a wren scourging
a gap in the hedge
and I'm back that afternoon
pruning clematis
where it fingered sky
at the Bramley's tips.

'Sweet-and-sour', you'd said,
remember, planting it there
under the cankered tree,
young roots tracing old,
puddling them in.

It was a wren bullied
the blood-red sun
that afternoon, secateurs
keen as the bird's fiat;
pain, bitter-sweet, just
this side of fainting;
a pistachio of fingertip —
somewhere my prints on the soil —
and spent coins of blood
up the garden path
to the kitchen sink.
Two months and more
Tipp-exed misprints,
nine-finger typing.

Squeals of a snatching brake,
or a wren chivvying
summer rain:
Mrs. Cholmondeley, pale blue
bleeding to mauve,
crêpe fingering sky again.

Comforts

Come back soon to a real Bridlington welcome
—noticeboards on the main roads out.

Those holidays, our nineteen-twenties
parents freed us here, their skinny kids
in handknit woollen swimsuits —
crotches like anglers' landing-nets —
peeing a catch of seawater
between sun-toughened knees;
and schooldays following, bubblegums
of skin peeled from our shoulders
pagefuls of rubbings-out.
Retirement brought us back to spend
the nineties, perhaps to close our book
in the comfort of this place.

But now we find that holidays
mean all the parking spaces filled;
we're jostled off the pavements
by macro-bosoms from McGill,
ogled by Cyclops beer-guts,
leered at by anal cleavages
escaping from Bermudas;
we're tripped by men in sandals
and obligatory black socks;
there's cellulite in armfuls here
and all the very ones who 'really shouldn't'
force-feed each other burgers.

From Sheffield, Bradford, Barnsley most,
the locals call them Comforts, for the way
they say they've 'come for t'day'.
And when they've 'done us brass' and driven off
westward past the come-back signs —
to the wife's part-time, the old man's emphysema —

what they leave behind for us
(discounting all the parking bays
of dunked-out teabags, disposables and stubs)
is the comfort of a season's end
in open space, the scour of rough seas
and the culling winds of winter.

Lessons In Age

We sit in facing chairs and share an hour
or so of silence, then both speak at once
our thoughts — 'I'll put the kettle on.' 'I'll draw
the curtains.' — or reel off some household tip:

'A bunch of rhubarb leaves brought to the boil
will clean stained pans as good as anything.'

'To change a fuse-wire, first switch off the mains —
and don't forget the torch that's hanging there
should have its batteries renewed each year.
The fuseholder with white spots is for lights —
5 amps — the thinnest fuse-wire on the card.'

So much to learn; so much to leave behind.
Against the time one's left to sit alone
we've planned our strategy, reversing roles
to learn each other's skills.

                              'For smooth white sauce
first make a roux: a knob of margarine,
a saucepan on low heat, the cooking-spoon
of cornflour — not too heaped, mix to a paste;
add milk, bring gently ... well, you know the rest,
but keep on stirring — use the whisk — you'll feel
the thickening in time.'

                    And when our time
is up, no doubt they'll say we blended well,
and so we do, but we have problems too —
well, don't we all? Compatibility
does not come cheap, and this late in our lives
we daren't allow ourselves the luxury
of good old-fashioned rows — too great the risk
before we'd made it up time might be called.

'The wrench to turn the stopcock's in the space
below the sink—clockwise for *off*. Make sure
the central-heating boiler's switched off first.'

Our 1940's closer than last year
and love grows more demanding as we age:
protectiveness and bossiness encroach
to silt the veins where lust once ran in spate—

'Not with the teacloth—use the oven-gloves.'

'That way you'll hurt your back—lift from the knees.'

So much to leave behind; so much to learn.

Solstice

(i.m. E.D.)

Low-angled sun shines through our window and
the tinsel-decorated room glows bright
this shortest day. The photo in my hand
records a day of summer: you, in white

or off-white outfit, champagne shoes and bag,
sit, smiling, on the grass; below's the date
of nineteen-eightythree — before the drag
of wolflike illness bowed you with its weight.

The Christmas card (which brought this happy you,
your Michael kindly sent us so that we
remember you the way you'd want us to)
he's annotated, not with elegy

but with a celebration of your life
and of your poems read in Requiem,
of joyful times you'd shared as man and wife;
its scene depicts Christ's birth at Bethlehem,

a Tintoretto print, which might have been
precisely of your choice, as though you'd known
we'd need such crutch of hope on which to lean.
The card is signed in Michael's name alone.

Remnants

Another year to slough like an old suit
rancid with sweat and sundry spillages,
congealing loves, and hatreds undeclared;
baggy from overnighting with intent
where dreams disintegrate in face of dawn —
and just becoming comfortable, warm.

With each year-end we play out this charade
as though some evil curse would strike us down
if, just for once, we dared sneak off to bed
and leave the old clothes crumpled on the floor
before the minute-hand eclipsed the hour-
hand's upright poise. And so we catnap here

a last few hours, for auld lang syne. The box
repeats repeats long past their drowse-by date —
climactic highlights, schmaltz and instant-sex
and holidays abroad we can't afford,
then rendezvous with Scotland and the malt,
the kilts that leave us cold, bagpipes that don't —

until, due deference done to Hogmanay,
past midnight we switch off the set, undress,
let fall the good old days, shrug off the bad,
but don't discard them all: a few we'll keep
like scraps of tweed cut off with pinking-shears,
and buttons saved from cast-offs through the years.

Pillow-talk

It troubles me how, recently
we've grown

apart, and don't now share,
as once we did,

that perfect empathy
we made our own

in so relaxed a way.
I cannot rid

my mind of fears and doubts
which come between

us now.
You seem so distant when I try

to reach you;
it's as though somehow I've been

rejected, bypassed,
and I don't know why.

Our intimacy's lately lost
all zest

and when we touch
it's only for a little while —

I can't remember when
we two caressed

in any lasting way.
Please make me smile

again, for old time's sake,
please say you'll keep

a tryst, and share my bed tonight,
dear Sleep.

Autumn Lodge—The Dayroom

They try to read beyond each other's eyes
but only see a face's fallen shape,
the balding eyebrows and the nasal hair,
the fissures of a deeply sculpted frown,
the corners of a mouth slow-arcing down;

each sees in each the portraiture of age
beyond her own, and wonders how it feels
to be as frail as one across the room
who, standing now, extends an arm to me
and helps me from my chair, and in to tea.

The Watchers

'La vita di quel mare era come le sorti infinite degli uomini, eternamente ferme in onde uguali,
mosse in un tempo senza mutamento'.
—Carlo Levi, Cristo si è fermato a Eboli.

Not your fresh, kindly breeze from Dalmatia
to wrinkle the drowsing Adriatic's back;
theirs a swingeing blast bringing Bergen
and the North Sea beating up the shore
to their anchorage, when winter comes.

Ancona. Bridlington. The eternal sea
locked to the call of the sun and the moon,
mirror to the infinite sky and mimic of clouds;
thwarted old age raging against the harbour quoins,
spitting with the wind when it comes, vehement.

There was rage, too, throughout constricted youth
moving in a time that seemed without change;
and it is change that they rage against now
their bodies impose new demands and routines
and the teacup shakes in their hand.

Only the unpeopled prom intervenes
between the Retirement Home and the sea;
watchers beside their windows drowse.
Their sea this dreary, autumn afternoon
no more than a slurp at a saucer of tea.

How will they ride out the waves, these old ones?
Locked in their slack, perpetual neap
will they pray for one final pull of the moon,
a low spring tide and a cleanswept shore
and watch for the coming of Christ? We shall see.

Ex Libris

Have you seen them, the silly old chumps?
If the library opened at dawn
they'd be there with their coughs and their limps
a good fifteen minutes before.

Have a look how they queue at the door
ten minutes to opening-time,
date-stamped and dog-eared and worn
like the books they're about to return.

Their addiction to standing in queues
was born in their boring old war:
up the blue, for their soyas and 'V's;
on the Home Front, for something to wear.

It's a kind of group statement they make —
it's not only for books that they come —
standing here they are making their mark,
being noticed, a someone, a name.

There's a nexus slipped out of their lives
and they seek to recapture it here
swapping wartime exploits and lost loves —
all that bull about *esprit de corps*.

When the door is unbolted at ten,
like good soldiers they'll pick up their bags,
put their war snaps away and file in
to search for their dead in new books.

A Kind Of Kindness

We talk again of death, of what it means
to die, and where we hope that death might lead—
and here at once I have to take a stance:
with no religious faith in afterlife
I see death only as an end of strife.

My fears are not about the void beyond;
what troubles me is all in death's approach:
dementia, pain, and physical decline,
incontinence, and needing help to dress.
Death, please come swift—a sudden nothingness.

O Tempora! O Mores!

Girls bursting out
from Headlands High
are switched on,
plugged in to
themselves.
A peripatetic
takes it out
on his clutch
and blitzes
his sunroof
with bassbeat.

It's all *pleases* and *pardons*
in our pensioners' cafe
and muzak restful
as the *Jesu Joy* of the Crem;
a hearing-aid howls now and then.
Nobody's looking
but everyone's watching
the couple who've lingered
too long at the one window table.
When they stand up to leave
it's Klondike.

A View Of The Sea

(Las Cascadas, Puerto de Andraitx, Majorca)

Steep, you'd have to call this coastline;
the houses, grafted to the island's bone,
white as gulls' wings, except when seen
from a gull-high view: oven-hot peach

and terracotta pantile roofs
cascade to the cool of the sea.
It is good, like watching others at work,
to gaze, from this honeysuckled balcony,

upon comings and goings below, although
the boats are too far off to be peopled
like the houses ashore. From my seat
in a slant of shade I become absorbed.

Garrulous in second, a Volkswagen grows
slowly bigger up the terraced hill, pulls
into position centre-stage, and stops;
the engine clears its throat, then dies.

Car doors open—his and hers—and shut
with a positive Doppelpunkt:
they walk to the rear as to part
wordless, hesitate, turn, touch hands

and kiss, lightly, their bodies held
apart—I can see the sea between.
Watching them their separate ways
I'm left to guess their story.

Whatever, they will both live it out
unknowing my concern, not even caring.
My theories cascade to the pull of the sea,
compelling, misting now, indeterminate.

Moment In History

(Chesters, Hadrian's Wall, 1992)

All day he smothers her with lore —
has done for years. Now it's *Cilurnum*,
stone footings of a Roman fort,

carved gulleys, good-luck phallus.
Drowns her now with pleasures,
all imagined, in The Baths ...

Frigidarium ...
> *Tepidaria* ...
>> *Caldaria* ...

She doesn't hear. She's sloughing
the wersh remains of him,
awaiting her moment to tell ...

... not here, in the peopled museum,
his hymning the glass-cased remains
and chanting aloud to found stones:

... millefiori brooch ... jet ring ...
snaffle bit ... entrenching tool ...
To the goddess Fortuna, Conservatrix ...

They'll take English tea on a bench
in the afternoon sun and she'll tell
of her lover. He'll jet back

alone to Tacoma.

Skulls At Phnom Penh

The road here reaches
back from the grave,
man-laid, each cobble
stares you out
from its two dark vaults.

No need of necromantic art
to bring alive
the unspoken words.
The cobbles whisper,
conch-like, in the wind:

you could have cared;
you should have cared.

Once More, On War

1. GAME CALL

Best part of half a century since last
we'd met. Old Corporal Barry he was then
to us young soldiers; must have been at least
twelve years my senior, an ancient man,

survivor of Tobruk, Sidi Rezegh—
those battles that the wireless used to name
and we'd seen spelt out in the local rag—
Gazala, Fort Capuzzo, Bir Hakeim.

Such place-names filled our conversations then
before I was myself posted abroad
to join his unit under canvas on
the desert's edge near Cairo. As I said,

not far off fifty years and now I faced,
just by the baker's shop in my new town,
a man I thought I recognized—the eyes
perhaps, or something of the nose, then soon

the angle of his head convincing me
I knew him from somewhere. He showed no sign
of recognition, so, reluctantly
I passed him by—but turned to look again

and saw a walk that leapt across the years,
a march I knew I first fell in behind
at Beni Yusef, with the IVth Hussars.
I rushed back—'Barry!', offering my hand

but even though he shook it in return,
he couldn't place my name, nor did my face
strike chords. He'd 'stopped one in the Gothic Line',
(I knew) 'and can't remember much these days.'

'The Regiment, and Colonel Kidde (Sunray),
Lance Sergeant Dunne ...' and some before my time
he could recall, but not remember me,
remustered Driver/Op fresh out from home,

until I asked him did he still play Bridge,
(we'd once played partners). Well, that took the trick—
the Slam was on!—with 'Charlie Ryde ... Bill Budge ...'
an outspread groundsheet, and that grubby pack.

2. SNAKES IN SICILY

The skin once scratched, old desert-sores began
once more to itch, and so we met again
and told conflicting versions of events;
compared the turns our lives had taken since.

He showed me photographs. On two of them
I could identify myself for him
and name some others he could not recall.
He had some German photographs as well,

he'd 'found them in a Jerry, a Mark Three,
shot-up outside—let's think—Mersah Matruh':
a group of Panzer troops; a girl back home
in German snow—we couldn't say her name,

but could read *Schlangen auf Sizilien*
written in ink on the reverse of one
cracked photograph. These snakes in Sicily
evoked that snake which came one hot, hot day

to drink while Lawrence at his water trough
stood like a second-comer, wondering if
his fear, or fear of being cowardly
would make him kill the drinker where it lay;

these half a dozen dead snakes in the dust
seemed somehow symptomatic of war's waste,
of chances missed. I'd say Lawrence was right—
here, too, was pettiness to expiate.

More than a month now and the dreams persist
of troops and tanks, and bodies in the dust;
I, in pyjamas, have the killing-stick,
the fear, the cowardice, a drinking snake.

All Down The Avenue

All down the avenue the houses make
bold statements, fantasize: first, Number 2,
with scarlet lamps and phallic Irish yew,
proclaims *Retirement Home For Gentlefolk*.

Then, over by the disused petrol pump
there's *Vindolanda*, double-glazed and lagged:
clearly the house is old, its ridgepole sagged,
but nothing here suggests a Roman camp.

Greengables lies a midlength terrace-house.
Next-door's *The Lindens*: not a lime in sight,
unless we count the floodlighting at night;
(that half-shut stable-door's not for a horse).

Cartref, oh, yes, *Cartref*! You're sure to meet
a *Cartref* every hundred homes or so:
St. David's songs left this one years ago
when Mamgu's health declined in Pontypridd.

Broadacres! What imaginative flair
led to the christening of 26,
whose aspect offers only others' bricks
plus, on a cloudless day, St. Mary's spire?

How precious are the dreams which move the mind
to sublimate what's ugly, bland or trite;
yet time might prove the incomers were right
renaming *Sunrise Cottage*: *Journey's End*.

Half-Term

An hour into our shopping trip I flag,
my threshold reached, and leave her to her quest
for 'something colourful but not too young,
to wear to next month's golden wedding do',
escaping to this seat out in the mall.

Here, while my wife re-racks the whole boutique,
I sit and watch the well-dressed shoppers pause
to gaze in windows, some at the displays
and some to titivate their scarf or hat
or satisfy a narcissistic need.

And if you've ever wondered what goes on
inside the heads of men who sit on seats
and ogle passers-by, come, sit with me,
it's marvellous — fantastic's more the word!
I choose at will, make this one rich, that poor —

they run a Merc or Mini at my whim;
this man's done time; that woman's on the stage;
he, in the Crombie, hosts a pheasant shoot;
she's not his wife; this rather plump girl sings
contralto; and this one ... this is my wife —

she hasn't bought a dress. 'Couldn't decide
between the paisley two-piece and a warm
more serviceable jersey-cloth. Half-term,
you see', she says, 'the shops are full of kids
whose mothers let them do just as they like

and I get flustered, then can't concentrate.
We'll come again, when schools are back ...', she jerks
me back into the school of mundane thought —
and this ménage à trois, that unfrocked priest,
this fool, re-metamorphose and move on.

Only Connect

for John Lucas

One canvas calls
whenever I'm in Hull:
lack-literate,
I'm drawn to Bundy's *School*

ceilinged in smoke
and dole of candlelight
where workworn men
first learn to read and write;

one sits alone,
looks apprehensive, grim
and out of place:
I see myself in him

and can't equate —
a century ahead —
my workthrift years
with all the books unread.

My passion primed,
I reach to you and send
a postcard print
and you respond, 'Dear friend,

this brush speaks well
alongside Tawney's pen!
Enclosed: his words.'
The lamps are lit again.

The Hull Poets — And Pigeons

'... the third generation Hull poets are proving worthy inheritors of the Larkin-Dunn estate.'
—John Osborne on *The Hull Poets*, Lincolnshire & Humberside Arts' *Arts Diary*
Jan–Feb 1987.

But few of them are native to the town,
most came by chance, or maybe second choice
and some have taken off with good degrees;
others fillet fish, or sign for dole.
One I know who flew the nest southwards
is honoured now, well-known and widely read
but yet unclaimed by Hull, his native town.
Such recognition isn't easily
obtained in Hull — the opportunity
might come with death: few Hullites there can be
who're unaware of Marvell's old complaint
to his coy lady, voiced by Humber's tide
above the sound of time's winged chariot;
but fewer still will know that Stevie Smith
lived here her early, valuable years.

Hull City Hall's a favoured pigeon squat
and Queen Victoria's monument is not
amused by small excretions, year on year;
by columnists and poets home to roost,
perhaps to earn, in time, the town's acclaim,
be granted all the privilege and pomp
the Three Crowns coat-of-arms would guarantee;
but clap your hands in Queen Victoria Square —
indigenous pigeons take to the air,
while alien poets are named as legatees
to Halls of Residence in Cottingham
and Bransholme's sprawling council house estates.
It matters not at all from where they came,
the pigeons or the poets; *poems* remain —
well, some — and pigeon-muck accumulates.

Were I a pigeon I'd have lost my strut,
revisiting a Humberside library,
to find my own slim volume credited
not to me, *Maurice*, but to *Margaret*,
denying me, whilst not my place of birth,
my rightful gender — hitting where it hurts —
(and Margaret's fame required no boost from me!).
And so I doubt Hull's City Fathers will
remark the passing of one *Rutherford*,
son of a Hull fish curer's manager
and writer of occasional short verse,
but should you see, one day, a chequered-blue
chance-bred streeter, in weak iambic flight,
homing on Hull like some lost poem recalled,
make room along the ledge — and let it land.

Lime Street To Paragon

(returning from a meeting with poets)

Slowing for Batley
I'm reading a poem
of someone who'd fallen
asleep on a journey
reading a poem.

The poem was dreaming
a poem of someone
who'd fallen asleep in
a poem unwritten

till slowing for Batley

woke me.

On Saving The Non-Winners Pile For Re-use As Draft-Paper

Some became almost friends
you wouldn't want to lose;
but some were just too nice
to be believed.

One wore pale pink—and didn't wash.

The weaker ones brought sick-notes
they'd salvaged from Eng. Lit.,
or piggybacked on Old Masters.

Some had been allowed too slack a rein, taken the bit and
over-run.

A few had been on courses
for advanced assertiveness.

Some weren't decided on a form
until halfway, then limped home in
iambics and tetrameters.

One, acrobatic, did handstands
& leapfrogged over ampersands.

Among first persons singular
one towered over all the rest
by sneaky use of lower-case.

Time warp incarcerated some
in outworn cloaks and hats of yore
to twixt and tween lost schooldays o'er.

Still more were cut by scattered shards
and bled in rosebay willowherb
or plashed through skeins of gossamer
to where they all arrived to meld
poetical as palimpsest.

The Reading

His beard has practised
all week without a comb.
He shuffles through
a well-thumbed sheaf
of poems — massed

endpapers for the one
he's brought to read.
Selfish with his foreplay
he describes
his poem's conception,

relives its long gestation.
All, then, that remains
is for him to read the thing.
Listen, and you'll hear
Movement, Dylan, Martian,

then, somewhere hereabouts
he finds for what it's worth
the voice he likes
to call his own ...
now, coming

to his *coup de grâce*
he hones to bare bone
colloquial modernity,
no skulker behind euphemism
he; but he fails

by eschewing the use
of a northern 'u' as in duck,
both vowel and impact weaken
pronounced more like quack.
The poem is born deformed.

His friend in the fourth row
slaps it into life;
motherless it cries
for sympathy and understanding.
Catharsis is complete.

The beard leads its poet
off the stage.
They'll ask you
what it was he read.
You won't remember.

Dear Mr. George

'It would be idle to claim that this pupil's record in most subjects is all that an educational institution would desire, but he has done very careful and good work in Typewriting. This suggests that he has a leaning towards the practical rather than the theoretical side of work. He will probably perform good service for an employer, and I know from experience that he will always be courteous, and regular and punctual in attendance.'
—Allan F. George LL.B., B.Sc. (Econ.) Lond.
Principal, City of Hull College of Commerce.
12th April, 1938.

Dear Mr. George, your words are with me yet,
outlasting fully fifty years in which
I've, probably, performed good services
for more than one employer, none of whom
I deigned to show your Testimonial.

It would not be at all idle to claim
that irony is what you taught me best,
its theory and its practical effects,
its gift in turning language on itself—
(Mark Antony might well have learned from you!).

Ironic in my turn, I now confess
the youth you labelled 'always courteous'
was that coarse wit who, in Assembly Hall,
would parody your 'Pirates of Penzance'
with lewd libretti, lavatorial.

Poetic too, I turned my back on school
a term before my time, to take a job
(without recourse to you as referee)
and thus confirmed pragmatic tendencies
yet gave the lie to your 'attendance' sop.

But that's all in the past; I've since returned
to your beloved Palgrave's Wordsworth, Keats,
discovered Larkin, Brownjohn, Harrison —
whose 'V' I love as much as you would loathe —
and seen my own two volumes into print.

Should ever anybody ask me who
most influenced my work (though this assumes
the questioner had read me — and few do)
I'd own a major debt to you, and quote
this damning, treasured Testimonial.

Dear Mr. George, your irony still stings
as, carefully, I send new poems out
and, regularly, get them back again
from publishers whose pulse-rate must have peaked
were Typewriting the sole criterion.

Bolt For Freedom

for Matt Simpson — and all gatecrashers

'The purpose of poetry is to remind us
how difficult it is to remain just one person,
for our house is open, there are no keys to the door,
and invisible guests come in and out at will.'
—Czeslaw Milosz

There now, it's done. I've bolted all my doors.
I've had it up to here being strung along
by poet puppeteers. Enough's enough.
I've raged against the dying light too long,
and cannot count how often drowned, not waved;

and what of all the times you've had me out
from daybreak drooling on that bloody bridge
at Westminster! I've got more urgent calls
to spend my days on: shopping; plants to pot;
and letters won't just write themselves, you know.

The peace you promised me on Innisfree
I failed to find. No, dropping bombs on Slough
was more my trip; cathartic, that, like when
you sent me with my aerosol to Leeds,
So, right, yer buggers, then, I thought, 'Cop this!'

My character's irrevocably changed—
I'm sure your lolly-stick did me no good!
And yet, fool that I am, I stayed to make
the cocoa for Old Wotsizname. But why,
so late in life, *the must of all those books?*

How mean, the stunt you pulled in '55,
and, knowing I don't smoke, you might have cleared
that saucerful of stubbed-out fags away
before you had me lie on Bleaney's bed —
and, anyway, those curtains drove me mad!

So far, I've humoured you. Not any more.
You're lousing up my biorhythmic flow —

— and if you think you'll get me, one more time,
to perch up in that fifth tier with my oar
and bust a gut to row your bloody tub
of ivory and peacocks all the way
from Ophir ...
                    Boy! Have I got news for you!

Recapture

I'd thought to free myself; that I should stay
out of your reach behind my bolted doors
and, there, to help in keeping you at bay
I concentrated on the household chores.

I spring-cleaned all the rooms and paid some bills —
the bathroom tiles have never shone so white.
My health improved, the doctor cut my pills
down to the knock-out two I take each night.

(If nicotine, booze, junk, sex, Tarot cards
and poetry are all addictive, I
had now one pressing need: renounce all bards!)
So, Wystan, Franceses, Johns, All — Goodbye!

Sometimes, I must admit, whilst dusting shelves
I'd feel the slightest tingle — nothing worse —
the one when suddenly we sense ourselves
observed — so skipped the shelf containing verse.

And during all this time, well shot of you,
released from all your hectoring I felt
so marvellously ME! I little knew
you'd stoop to hitting me below the belt.

Not quite below the belt—let's be precise,
more when my guard was down — but was it right
or gallant of you to exact your price
for one slip in my watchfulness, one night?

It happened when the children were asleep:
I'd just looked in, the way that parents will,
to see them safe and, whilst there, paused to peep
outside, between the curtains and the sill,

and that act brought back Bleaney's room once more —
one wayward thought, and liberty was lost!
But what recaptured me was what I saw:
the *moonlight lying on the grass like frost.*

The doors sprung wide — my dream of freedom ends
with, *on the highest pavement of the stair,*
the *wheelbarrow* on which *so much depends;*
that *silk hat on a Bradford millionaire.*

Mr. Larkin

This was Mr. Larkin's bike. He rode
it all round Hull and Holderness, until
his need to scarper faster from the toad
egged him to motoring. And look, it still

bears scars and rust-pox down the near front fork
where he fell off, that night returning home
half-drunk on *Which* and washing sherry talk
from Warlock-Williams' do. On it he'd comb

the lanes of Patrington, Sunk Island, Paull,
in search of—what? An iffy tanner left
as conscience-geld in some church plate? Of all
that time torn off unused: those days bereft

of poems; nights starved of sex? Or did he look
for what he'd never found in booze and bars,
nor teased out from the pages of a book;
something he'd left at home, perhaps? That vase?

It's dodgy ground, I know, to say these trips
away from cut-price crowds spelt more of gain
than loss, to claim he wrote from cycle clips
as profitably as he did by train.

But if he thought, death-suited, swerving east
back from some Lit-bore London interlude,
that here in Hull was where it mattered least
what foreign poets said; shivered, and viewed

'abroad' as inhospitable, cold, dark;
and slowing into Paragon he'd glow
with hope that not too far from Pearson Park
he'd find a new Parnassus, I don't know.

This Be The Curse

I fucked them up, my Mum and Dad;
I didn't mean to, but I did
by cropping up late, when they'd had
their seventh and, they'd thought, last kid.

But they fucked me up in my turn
by handing their libido down
and setting me on course to earn
repute as Randiest Buck In Town.

My life's one endless ding-a-ling—
What, me, complaining? I'm no fool—
until Mum's voice calls up to bring
me down from dreams, and late for school.

Rome Is So Bad

Rome is so bad. Wartime, I thought it fine,
a place to come, see, conquer, then stay on.
So why did chaps like Hadrian take the line
forsaking lives of lust, and turn for fun
to humping stone from Solway to the Tyne?

Was it religion limited their scope?
Like when, a virgin squaddie, I found sex:
the Via Nuova, Carla—paid in soap
and fags—her bed beneath the crucifix,
Madonna watching from the wall. That pope.

The Autumn Outings

That autumn, I was quick getting away:
      only about
one-twenty on the rain-drenched Wednesday
I locked the premises and motored out,
all staff sent home, all workshop plant closed down,
all sense of any kind of business gone,
and not until I'd driven fifteen miles
along fast-flooding roads back into town,
past rival complexes just clinging on,
did rain let up and vision clear: those files

I'd never see again; that desk, the phone
      that shrilled all day
when first it was installed; not hear the moan
compressors made, be soothed by lathes, nor say
'Good morning George, alright?', or 'Nice one, Bert',
the human touch, no more, not to distract
them too long from their work, but just enough
to let them see I cared, and not to hurt
old feelings as I tried to breast the fact
of cancelled orders, creditors turned rough.

The friendly bank soon bared its teeth — drew blood;
      and then that bane,
the Tax Man, claimed his pound. And so, the flood.
(Fine detail dims again as, too, the pain
recedes three autumns on; yet loss stays true.)
The rain comes vicious now — wipers full speed,
dipped headlights on, rear fogs — the journey seems
to lengthen every time I live it through,
involuntarily, as when the need
for sleep is scuppered by recurring dreams.

My crowd was breast-fed clichés, meal on meal:
      to pull its weight,
nose to the grindstone, shoulder to the wheel,

and, once it stepped inside the factory gate,
was wedded to its work; slapped all the time
by Newbolt's hand: *Play up, and play the game.*
Well, this sounds fine; but what about the bloke
who's anorexic, short-nosed, cannot climb
to reach the wheel, and never makes the team?
For him such wedding tales are guffs of smoke.

Again the morning paper hits the floor —
      banner headlined:
PIT CLOSURES SHOCK — and umpteen thousand more
are facing broken marriages to mines.
A few, lured by that bit-of-fresh, fool's gold,
pin hopes on boarding-houses, market stalls;
one man sits out his protest down the pit,
while lefties call for strikes with all the old
clenched-fist salutes, and aerosol the walls:
SCARGILL FOR KING and TARZAN IS A SHIT.

Their first few days of idleness will see
      in those it hits
undreamt-of traits in personality:
some will get by and others go to bits;
the strong become the weak, the weak make good
as quickly as it's said. Then, as the days
stack up to months or, as in my case, years,
high principles get trampled in the mud
where guile and self-survival point new ways
to quick back-pocket jobs, fiddles, and fears

of being caught. But fears will yield, in time,
      a sort of pride,
though not the social pride that saw men climb
from old-world swamps: a sense that one's defied
the odds, the system; finger-licked the crème,
nose-thumbed some top brass, bested those who made
the rules and all the running. What survives?
Of Us: too early yet to tell. Of Them:

'Indifferents and Incapables'; their trade
in UB40s and P45s.

In brass-lined boardrooms up and down the land
        deep in regret
a million more redundancies get planned,
while chairmen's hiked-up salaries are set,
and Urban Councils chase arrears in rents.
Wideboys, insider-dealers, some M.P.s
grow richer by a second home in Spain,
a custom-plated white Mercedes-Benz,
that new portfolio. True-blue disease.
The spores of loss, somewhere becoming gain.

October, 1992

Postscript To My Father

'Über Sternen muss er wohnen'
—Friedrich Schiller, 'An die Freude'

Those not-forgotten soured days, the booze-
blitzed nights, dawn absences — the man I knew
but mostly didn't. Dad, tonight I choose
to break with these and find a later you,

the one I took to golf, saw home again
drunk on the laughter of a fluked par-three,
and baited-up for, once on Hedon Drain —
work-knackered, dragging your redundancy —

that time you grassed a 2-ounce roach and caught
the smit, remember? Lately, those few days
snatched in maturity return — hard-bought,
the bill paid in advance. If there were ways

of reeling-in snagged lines to cast again
in new-found swims, could you or I resist?
Some unfished pool: who knows what specimen,
what sport, what joy! This time the catch not missed

like football in the park or Guy Fawkes Night,
the conkering we never got to share
or subtleties of keeping-up a kite …
Those got away before. Dad, if I dared

believe you'd found an afterlife, I'd wish
—no, pray — this postscript reach you there above
tonight's brief stars: I know a stream, a fish
which, lured, hooked and landed, could be love.

NOTES

The epigraph on the dedication page is from John Donne's '*The Good-Morrow*'.

BITTER ALOES (page 12)
Bitter aloes: a tincture to deter nail-biting.

TUTORIAL (page 15)
The tune: *When I Grow Too Old To Dream*.

SOLSTICE (page 26)
E.D. suffered *lupus erythematosus*.

THE WATCHERS (page 31)
The quotation from '*Christ Stopped At Eboli*' might translate: 'The life of that sea was like the interminable lot of the people, eternally locked in monotonous waves, moving in a time without change.'

EX LIBRIS (page 32)
up the blue: in the desert (W.W.2.)
soyas: sausage substitutes.
'*V*'s: free-issue cigarettes.

ALL DOWN THE AVENUE (page 41)
Cartref: home.
Mamgu: Grandma.

ONLY CONNECT (page 43)
Edgar Bundy's *The Night School*, (1892), Ferens Art Gallery, Hull.
R.H. Tawney's *An Experiment In Democratic Education*, (1914), Political Quarterly.
'Only connect the prose and the passion, and both will be exalted, and human love will be seen at its highest.'—E.M. Forster, *Howards End*.